KING JOASH

Book 4

A CHILD'S BIBLE KIDS

Katheryn Maddox Haddad

Northern Lights Publishing House

Cover design by Sharon Lavy &
Jim Pagett, Images licensed by
Sweet Publishing http://sweetpublishing.com
Copyright © 2017 Katheryn Maddox Haddad

ISBN-978-1-948462-03-7

All rights reserved, including the right to reproduce this book or portions thereof in any form.
No part of this book may be reproduced, stored, transmitted, or distributed in any form or by any means
without prior written permission from the author.
The only exception is for a brief quotation in a printed review.

Printed in the United States.

NOTE: The author used mostly one-syllable words. Longer words were sometimes hyphenated
to help the child pronounce them.

Other Books By this Author For All Ages

HISTORICAL NOVELS
Series of 8: They Met Jesus
Ongoing Series of 8: Intrepid Men of God
Mysteries of the Empire with Klaudius & Hektor
Christmas: They Rocked the Cradle that Rocked the World
Series of 8: A Child's Life of Christ
Series of 10: A Child's Bible Heroes
Series of 8: A Child's Bible Kids
Series of 10: A Child's Bible Ladies

HISTORICAL RESEARCH BIBLE
for Novel, Screenwriter, Documentary & Thesis Writers

TOPICAL
Applied Christianity: Handbook 500 Good Works
Christianity or Islam? The Contrast
The Holy Spirit: 592 Verses Examined-
The Road to Heaven
Inside the Hearts of Bible Women-Reader+Audio+Leader
Revelation: A Love Letter From God
Worship Changes Since 1st Century + Worship 1sr Century Way
Was Jesus God? (Why Evil)
365 Life-Changing Scriptures Day by Date
The Road to Heaven
The Lord's Supper: 52 Readings with Prayers

FUN BOOKS
Bible Puzzles, Bible Song Book, Bible Numbers

TOUCHING GOD SERIES
365 Golden Bible Thoughts: God's Heart to Yours
365 Pearls of Wisdom: God's Soul to Yours
365 Silver-Winged Prayers: Your Spirit to God's

SURVEY SERIES: EASY BIBLE WORKBOOKS
→Old Testament & New Testament Surveys
→Questions You Have Asked-Part I & II

Genealogy: How to Climb Your Family Tree Without Falling Out
Volume I & 2: Beginner-Intermediate & Colonial-Medieval

Table of Contents

Other Books By this Author For All Ages iii

1 ~ Baby Prince 1
2 ~ Running 9
3 ~ Escape 17
4 ~ Hiding 24
5 ~ Growing 32
6 ~ Almost King 40
7 ~ Practicing 47
8 ~ Telling the Secret 55
9 ~ All the Guards 62
10 ~ Long Live the King 71

Thank You 80
Buy Your Next Child's Book Now 81

About the Author 82
Connect with the Author 83

Get a Free Book 84
Join My Dream Team 84

1 ~ Baby Prince

"Our new king is gone again," the high priest said to his wife.

"My brother has been king only a year. He needs to be here in Jerusalem," his wife, Princess Jeho-sheba said.

"He went off to war," the high priest said.

"He needs to be taking care of his

own kingdom. Besides, he has a young family at home," his wife said.

The two stop their conversation. They hear shouting.

"What's that noise out on the street?" the high priest asked as he rushed out of his home in the temple area.

His wife followed him down to the street.

"The king has been wounded! The king has been wounded!" one of the king's soldiers shouted, riding his horse through the streets of Jeru-salem.

The high priest stood in the middle

Book 4: King Joash

of the street, arms outstretched, to stop the soldier.

"Why are you not guarding your king?"

"The army fled after he was shot with that arrow."

"Where is he now?" the king's sister and high priest's wife asked. "I must get to him and help him."

"It is too danger-ous for him to return to Jeru-salem. He is escap-ing to another city. I do not know which one."

The high priest turned to his wife. "There is nothing we can do now except wait."

They returned to their home in the temple area. And waited for news of the king. They waited 1 day. 2 days. 3 days. 4 days.

"I must go see his family," Princess Jeho-sheba said. "If they heard he has been wounded, they will be worried."

She walked back through the temple area where her home was, then out a back gate to the palace next door.

When she got to the nursery, she looked around. "Where is little Joash?" she asked his nurse.

"He is sleeping, Princess Jeho-

Book 4: King Joash

sheba. All 1-year-old children sleep a lot. But he may be waking up about now."

Princess Jeho-sheba stepped into the sleeping room for the little prince. She watched him breathe as he dreamed baby dreams. She sat by his bed a while.

Suddenly, little Joash's eyes opened wide. He looked over to one side, saw his aunt, and smiled. He raised his head, then propped himself up and held out his little arms.

"Well, it is about time you woke up," Princess Jeho-sheba said, grinning and reaching over to pick up her nephew.

Joash giggled, then wiggled. She let him down on the floor and watched him crawl away to see what his little eyes could find to do.

"Isn't he walking yet?" the princess asked.

"He is too impatient," the nurse replied, laughing. "He does not know that, once he learns to walk, he can run and get places faster than crawling."

Princess Jeho-sheba heard shouting down on the street, just like the shouting a week earlier. She went to a window to hear better.

"Oh, no!" she said moments later

Book 4: King Joash

"Grab the baby! Run."

"Why? What has happened?" the nurse asked.

"Follow me!"

THINK & DO

1. Do you have an aunt or uncle who you have fun with? What is his or her name?

2. Draw a picture of you with them. Ask a grownup if they will help you send them the picture.

Book 4: King Joash

2 ~ Running

Princess Jeho-sheba rushed out to the hall of the palace. The nurse had Prince Joash in her arms.

Soldiers ran up and down the hall.

"I don't think the soldiers have been given their orders yet," she whispered to the nurse. "They don't know what to do."

Princess Jeho-sheba walked quickly

down one side of the hall, ducking behind statues whenever she saw one.

"What happened?" the nurse asked. The princes did not reply.

"I know where there is a secret passage-way," the princess said. "Stay close."

When they got to each statue, she pulled on the statue's hand. Finally, she came to the right one. When she pulled on its hand, a small square door in the floor behind the statue dropped open. There was a ladder under it.

"You and Joash go first," the princess urged. "Hurry."

Book 4: King Joash

The nurse obeyed. She handed Joash to his aunt, climbed down the ladder, then reached up for the prince.

As soon as the princess handed Joash back to his nurse, she hurried down the ladder herself.

The princess picked up the small square door, reached up, held it in place with one hand, and put a bar across it to hold it up. She could see the smallest hole of light where the thin rope ran from the bar to the statue's hand.

"Now, up in the hall above, it once again just looks like part of the floor," she said.

The princess turned around in the blackness.

"Just stand still. There are candles on a shelf along the wall near the ladder. Next to them is a bow-drill. My mother made me learn how to make fire with a bow drill when I was young. 'A princess never knows when she will have to escape in the dark,' she would always say."

Little Prince Joash began to cry.

"Oh, Princess Jeho-sheba," the nurse said, close to tears herself. "What if they hear him in the hall

Book 4: King Joash

overhead?"

"Don't worry. With all the shouting and stomping on the floor, no one will be able to hear."

By this time, the princess had found the bow-drill in the dark and was making enough sparks that the cotton ball next to it was smoking.

In the darkness, she picked up the cotton with the small flame and held it next to the wick of a candle.

Light came on in the dark tunnel. The princess took the candle and started down a passage-way.

The floor was dirt. The walls were dirt. It was a tunnel and very cold.

"Hurry," Princess Jeho-sheba said. "I am not the only one who knows about this secret passage way."

The princess and the nurse ran and ran in the tunnel.

At last, the nurse slowed down and gasped for air.

The princess turned around. "Hand Joash to me so you can catch your breath."

They ran and ran some more. Sometimes the tunnel turned to the

Book 4: King Joash

right. Sometimes it turned to the left. On, they ran. Farther. Farther. Farther.

The little prince began to cry.

"Don't be afraid, little one," the princess said as she continued to run. "We're just playing a little game."

But the tunnel stopped. Only dirty ahead and on both sides. They had reached the end. Where could they go? They were trapped.

A Child's Bible Kids

THINK & DO

1. Do you know what you would do if your house or apartment caught fire? Where would you run to? How would you escape? Talk to your parents about what you should do if there was a fire in your home.

2. Draw a picture of a house with flames in the window. Draw a ladder from the ground to the window. Draw a fireman or a fire truck on the ground. Write at the top or bottom of your picture, THANK YOU FOR SAVING US. Send the picture to a fireman.

Book 4: King Joash

3 ~ Escape

"We're not trapped, if that's what you're thinking," the princess said to the nurse.

She handed baby Joash back to the nurse and found a shelf along the dirt wall on which to set their candle.

Now they saw a ladder, just like there had been a ladder at the other end of the tunnel. She climbed half way up and knocked on the little door at the top of the ladder. They heard nothing. She yelled, "Anyone there?" No answer.

"I don't hear anyone up there," the princess said. "That is good. But we will open the door a little at a time just in case."

The princess took the bar with the little rope attached to it down. She let the little door in the floor above fall down.

She stuck her head out of the tunnel and looked around in the daylight.

"What in the world are you doing?" a gruff voice said.

Book 4: King Joash

"Oh, no!" the nurse called up. "We have been discovered."

The princess smiled. "No worries. It is just my husband, the high priest. We are in the temple area. Hand the prince up to me."

Princess Jeho-sheba passed the prince on up to her husband with a smile. "Whew! We made it."

She climbed out the rest of the way and turned to help the nurse up.

"You haven't heard?" she asked the high priest once they were fully out and the hidden door replaced.

"I guess not," she answered for

him. "The prince's father has died of his wounds. The enemy is bound to come after his family and capture them or worse."

"Hurry. Come with me," the high priest said with Prince Joash still in his arms. "We don't want any of the temple guards or other priests to see him."

The princess saw where someone had dropped a shawl while walking through the temple area. She picked it up and threw it over the head of Prince Joash.

"Wheee!" the prince called out from under the shawl. Then he giggled.

When they got to the house of the

Book 4: King Joash

high priest and princess, they rushed inside and closed the door.

When the princess took the shawl off her nephew's head, he wore a big grin. " 'gin," he said, " 'gin."

"We'll do that again another time," the high priest said, forcing a smile.

"Whew!" the princess said, leaning against a back wall with a hand over her fast-beating heart.

"Whew!" the nurse said, now on her knees on the floor. She looked up. "Would someone tell me what is going on?" she asked.

Prince Joash wiggled loose from the

high priest, got on the floor, and crawled over to his nurse.

The nurse sat up and took him in her lap.

"What is going on?" Princess Jehosheba repeated. "That little boy in your arms may be the next king."

Book 4: King Joash

THINK & DO

1. Did you ever own something that you never paid any attention to? Then one day you found out it was very valu-able? Maybe it was a special marble, or a ring, or an old toy. What did you do with it after you found out it was valuable?

2. What do you want to be when you grow up? You do not have to wait until you are grown up to be valu-able. You are valu-able to everyone who loves you right now.

Who in your life is valu-able to you? Draw a picture with a heart on it and give it to that person.

4 ~ Hiding

"The king?" Joash's nurse said, not knowing whether to believe them.

"His father, the king, will be buried in the cemetery of the kings here in Jeru-salem. Then a lot of people will be wanting to be the next king," the princess said.

The high priest looked at his wife, the princess. "He will be safe with us. Not many people come to worship at the

Book 4: King Joash

temple any more."

"Our great-great-grandfather, David would be ashamed of us all," Princess Jeho-sheba said. "You are so right. Hardly anyone comes to worship at the temple anymore."

"We have always had guards at our house since it is in the temple area," the high priest said, "so no one will think it strange that we have guards in the future."

One of the servants walked into the room and stopped in the doorway. Right away, the nurse threw the shawl back over the head of Joash. He giggled.

"Come with me," Jeho-sheba said.

She led the nurse with the baby down a long hall, up some back steps, then up some more steps to the top floor of their house.

"No one uses this top floor," she said to the nurse. "It will all be for you and the prince. You are never to leave here unless you are in disguise. Can you do that? He could be here for many years."

"I was always in the nursery at the palace and didn't go outside very often. Being here will not be much different," the nurse replied.

And, so, the wait began. Every day, the high priest came to see little Joash. Joash called him Uncky at first

Book 4: King Joash

but later called him Uncle when he could talk better.

On those visits, Uncle would teach him something about God.

"Did you know you are very special to God?" Uncle said one day. "You are special all the way up to the sky."

The high priest picked up Joash and let him reach as high as he could.

"Okay, let's sit," Uncle said. "Now, show me where your nose is."

Joash was smart and touched his nose.

"Good, now show me where your

ears are."

Joash showed him his ears.

"Let's practice walking now."

Joash showed the high priest how he could walk without someone helping him.

———

"I'm 2 years old," Joash said one day. "I'm big."

He ran everywhere and giggled where ever he went, especially if he found something he had never seen before.

Book 4: King Joash

There was now a queen in the palace nearby. She was not very nice. She bowed down to statues that were pretend gods. She didn't care. Her statues were pretty. Or they were handsome if they were boy pretend gods.

The high priest and his wife, the princess, kept Joash hidden on the 3rd floor of their big house in the temple area.

Servants were only allowed to be on the 1st floor of their house. The high priest and Jeho-sheba had children of their own. They had bedrooms on the 2nd floor of their house. Servants were not allowed to go on the 2nd or 3rd floor.

A Child's Bible Kids

Could little Joash stay hidden?

Book 4: King Joash

THINK & DO

1. If you could do anything you wanted for your next birthday, what would it be?

Here is an idea for you: For your birthday, make someone else feel special. It can be another child who people do not make friends with much, or a grownup. Cele-brate by getting two cupcakes and sharing them with that person.

Make someone else feel special on your birthday. Then you will feel special too.

5 ~ Growing

Then Joash was 3 years old. He learned to sing and liked it when his Uncle told him stories about his great-great-grandfather, King David.

"Sing Dabid, Sing Dabid," he said.

"Okay, what song about David would you like to sing?" the high priest asked.

Joash wagged his head back and forth. Then he said, "Bah, bah, bah."

Book 4: King Joash

So, they sang about David the shepherd boy, and at the end of each verse said, "Bah, bah, bah" like sheep.

Then Joash was 4 years old and still in hiding. But he did not know he was. He was too young still to understand.

He was talking whole sen-ten-ces now. "Let's run a race," he announced to his nurse sometimes. He loved it when his little legs went fast.

Then Prince Joash was 5 years old. He had been hiding in the same house ever since he could remember. It was his whole world.

"Why can't I ever go outside?" he was starting to ask whenever he looked out his window."

"Someday you will, little one," the high priest said.

"I'm not little, Uncle. I'm big."

"Yes, you are," the high priest replied. "And when you are just a little bigger, we're going to let you go outside."

Joash's eyes sparkled and he formed a wide grin. "The real outside?" he asked. "Not the roof outside?"

"Yes, the real outside. Then your life is going to change a whole bunch."

Book 4: King Joash

"Why?"

"Well, for one thing, you won't live here anymore. You know the big, big house next door to the temple? That is a palace. That is where you will live after you go to the real outside.

"Why can't I live there now?"

"Well, because there is a bad queen living there now. She is the daughter of the most wicked king and queen of the north who ever lived—King Ahab and Queen Jez-e-bel. She hurts people sometimes. We do not want her to hurt you."

"Will she move away so I can live in

the palace next door to the temple?"

The high priest did not reply.

"It is time you learn to write your name," he said. "I have brought a clay tablet and a brass stick."

"I can do that," Joash said.

"Okay, here is your name at the top. You practice copying the letters until you can write your name without looking where I wrote it. I will be back to-mar-row."

"Don't go away, Uncle," Joash said, crawling up into the high priest's lap. "Don't go away." A tear formed.

Book 4: King Joash

The high priest was surprised. Why was Joash sad? He was too little to be so sad.

"Joash, what is wrong?"

"What was my daddy like?"

"Oh, well, he was a great man. He was the king and everybody bowed down to him."

"Did he wear a crown?"

"Oh, yes. It was made of gold and very heavy."

"How heavy?"

"As heavy as a rock on your head,"

the high priest replied with a grin.

"As heavy as a chair on my head?" Joash giggled. "As heavy as a table on my head?"

"What are you 2 laughing about?" Princess Jeho-sheba asked, entering the room.

"We were talking about crowns," Joash announced.

"He knows?" she asked.

Book 4: King Joash

THINK & DO

1. Have you waited a very long time for something special to happen? What is it?

Is it a good idea to think about it all the time or just some of the time? Why?

2. Old people will tell you that the years of their young life flew by.

Draw a picture of a clock. On the clock, make bird wings. Put it in your room or on your re-frig-er-ator door. Remind yourself sometimes that, as you grow older, time will fly faster.

6 ~ Almost King

Little Joash was now 7 years old. For 6 of his 7 years he has been hiding.

For 6 long years, all day every day the only 3 people ever allowed to see Joash were his aunt the princess, his uncle the high priest, and his nurse.

Today was his birthday. They played games and had special food and sang songs.

Book 4: King Joash

That night as Princess Jeho-sheba kissed him goodnight, he began to cry.

"Why are you crying?" she asked.

"Because to-mar-row I am going to be lonely again," he said. "I see all the people down on the ground and I don't know anybody." His upper lip curled

She smiled. "Perhaps now is the time. I shall speak to my husband about it."

"About what, Aunt Jeho-sheba?"

"Your crown."

"I have a crown?" he asked.

"Go to sleep and we will talk some more to-mar-row."

With that, Jeho-sheba blew out the candle next to his bed and went down to the first floor of their house.

"Husband, the queen is getting meaner and meaner. I am ashamed of her," the princess said.

The high priest set down the book he had been reading. "Joash is 7 years old now. I have been teaching him the 10 Com-mand-ments and he knows them by heart."

"He is ready. Our kingdom is ready. Everyone is tired of the bad queen. They don't want her to be their queen

Book 4: King Joash

anymore," the princess said.

"To-mar-row, we begin preparing Joash to be king," the high priest, her husband, said.

———

Both the high priest and his wife, Princes Jeho-sheba went to the top floor of their house early the next morning. The nurse was not even awake yet.

Jeho-sheba patted Joash's long-time nurse on the cheek. "We want to wake him up this morning. From now on, he is going to be with us."

The nurse sat up in bed. "From now

on? Am I no longer his nurse?"

"You have done a wonderful job with him all these years. But, yes, very soon now, you will no longer be his nurse."

The princess thought a minute then add, "Unless, of course, you want to go with him to the palace. You will know him better than anyone there. Yes, you should go with him. But we need to prepare him now."

"Prepare him?"

"To be king."

Princess Jeho-sheba joined her husband in Joash's room. He had already awakened the boy.

Book 4: King Joash

"Really?" Joash was saying.

"How much have you told him, husband?" the princess asked.

"I'm going to be king," Joash said, his eyes bright. "And even more fun is that I won't be lonely any more. I can have all the friends I want. I can have 100 friends if I want. Isn't that right, Uncle?"

THINK & DO

1. Can you think of a time when you were surprised by something good happening? What was it?

2. Do you know someone who feels bad because they are lonely or got a bad grade in school or broke something? It could be any reason they feel bad.

Why don't you go see them or call them on the phone and surprise them with a song? What song would you like to sing for them?

Book 4: King Joash

7 ~ Practicing

"As soon as you are dressed, we want you to practice," Joash's aunt said.

"Practice what?"

"Wearing the crown."

"Is it as heavy as a rock?"

"Just about. Gold is very heavy."

Joash hurried into his clothes and took a few bites of bread and honey for his breakfast. "I'm ready to be king now," he said, standing with his arms straight down by his side. "Wow. Being king is going to be fun!"

"All right, King Joash, Your Majesty, here is your crown," the high priest said. "I will put it on you slowly so you can get used to the weight."

"Oh. I can't turn my head," Joash said as soon as the crown rested on his head. "If I do, it will fall off."

His aunt and uncle laughed.

"Don't make me laugh," Joash shouted. "You're going to make it fall

Book 4: King Joash

off."

He reached up when it began teetering to straighten it on his head.

"Now, try walking with it," Aunt Jeho-heba said.

He took a few steps. The crown teetered. "Oops" he said. He reached up and straightened it, and took a few more steps. "Oops, there it goes again."

The high priest stepped over and took the crown off.

"Okay, that's enough practicing with the crown for now," the princess said. "There are some people who are going to come here to help get you ready."

"Oh, goody," Joash said, dancing in a circle. "I'm already getting new friends."

"Well, they will have jobs to do. Once they come up here and see you, they will not be allowed to leave. We have set up cots in two rooms for them—one for the men and one for the women."

"That many?" Joash said. "Whoopie!"

"The tailor is due to be here any time now. He is going to make a purple robe for you," the high priest said. "Then there will be a shoe maker, and a barber, and..."

Book 4: King Joash

"Whew, you're wearing me out with all those people," Joash said with a wink.

"Oh, and there are going to be guards coming up here. They will follow you around."

"Every step?"

"Every step. They will not let you do some things you are used to doing such as going too close to the edge of the roof."

"It has a railing on it so high I can barely see over it," Joash replied.

"They will watch you eat, and watch

you sleep. You will never be alone again. Well, at least not for a long time."

They heard marching down on the ground below. The marching sound went away for a while, then came back. Temple guards entered the third floor.

"Reporting for duty, sir," the commander of the unit said.

He looked down at the boy. He had a hard time not looking at him. "Uh, sir, is this him? Is this the king that lived?"

"Yes, this is him," the high priest said, standing. "You will guard this boy with your life. He will soon be our king."

The old soldier pressed his lips hard

Book 4: King Joash

together. He sniffed. He was so happy their little king was still alive. He cleared his throat. With a trem-bling voice, he shouted, "Yes, sir! Yes, sir! Yes, sir!"

After that, he smiled at little Joash.

THINK & DO

1. Did you ever practice and practice and practice something so you could do it in front of other people? Then, you got nervous? You knew what you had to do because you had done it many times at home alone. But in front of other people, you weren't sure you were ready.

What can you tell your mind so you can do as well in front of other people as you do at home alone?

2. Memo-rize a verse in the Bible. Say it in front of other people.

Book 4: King Joash

8 ~ Telling the Secret

The high priest knelt in front of Joash who, for the first time in a long time, did not have anything to say. The boy had confusion in his eyes.

"Yes, this is what it is going to be like for you to be king. Do not be afraid. Be strong, my boy. Be strong. Make your father proud of you. Make King David proud of you. We are already proud of you."

With that, the high priest stood. "I will return later. While I am gone, I believe your aunt is going to show you what to say and do when people bow down to you."

"Bow down to me?"

The high priest hurried down the steps and out the front door of his house. There were 2 times more guards than usual. They saluted him.

He went to the building behind the temple used by the ruling Council of 70. His 5 most trusted friends—all captains of 100 soldiers each—were there. When he entered the room, he locked the door.

Book 4: King Joash

"You may wonder why I have sent for extra guards around my house. Men, what I am about to tell you has been a secret in the kingdom for 6 years. Once I tell you, you will say and do exactly what I tell you to say and do. Are you agreed? Do I have the vows of all of you?"

He looked around. Each of the 5 agreed.

"One of King David's great-great grandsons still lives."

The men in the room gasped in surprise.

"How?"

"Where?"

"My wife and I have been hiding him and his nurse in our house since the death of his father, the king. He was 1 year old at the time He is now 7 years old. He is ready. The kingdom is ready."

Silence. The 5 captains stared at the high priest, at each other, then back at the high priest.

"Now, this is what must be done," the high priest went on. "Go through the kingdom and bring back with you the elders of every city. I also want you to bring back with you every Levite servant of the temple. You have two weeks to get them back here to me. Do not tell

Book 4: King Joash

them why. Just tell them it is my command and must be obeyed.

The high priest unlocked the door and left.

Next, the high priest called some Levites serving at the temple to follow him to the arm-ory, the room King David kept spears and swords and shields for the temple guards long ago.

They had trouble getting the door open. "Are you sure this is the room you want, sir?" one of the Levite servants asked. "It doesn't look like it has been opened in 10 years."

"I am sure. Do what is necessary to break the lock and get the door opened."

At last, they were able to enter the room. They lit torches and looked around.

"Get the dust off them. Then polish tarnish off the silver so they shine like they should. Count them. Make sure there are enough spears and shields to go around."

"Enough for what, sir?"

"You will know soon enough."

With that, the high priest returned to his house and Joash.

Book 4: King Joash

THINK AND DO

1. Did your parents ever tell you to do something and you didn't want to because you didn't think it was important?

Maybe it was to clean up your room because overnight company was coming. Or maybe it was to help wash the dishes because you were going to get a surprise party.

Sometimes we need to trust older people when they tell us to do something. It may be more important than we think.

9 ~ All the Guards

"How are things going with our new king?" the high priest asked as he re-entered the third floor.

Joash rushed up to his uncle. "They are making a new purple robe just for me. And they gave me a cane with gold on top that I'm supposed to carry. And I practiced a long time wearing my crown. And…"

"You have been a busy boy," the

Book 4: King Joash

high priest said.

———

2 weeks went by fast for the high priest and his wife.

"Make sure Joash knows how to walk in his purple robe without tripping."

"Make sure Joash remembers the 10 Com-mand-ments."

"Make sure Joash can wear the golden crown without it falling off his head."

The time was finally here. "To-mar-row our little boy will no longer belong to just us, the high priest told his wife. "He will belong to his kingdom.

He will be their king."

The high priest went back down to the temple area. There he saw 100s of Levites and city elders who had been brought in from all over the kingdom just as he had commanded.

The high priest stood at the top of the steps leading to the altar where everyone could see him.

"What I am about to tell you men of Isra-el has been a secret until now," he shouted. "Before I tell you, you must swear to be loyal to who I tell you to honor."

Every man in the crowd raised his hand and shouted out his vow of loyal-

Book 4: King Joash

ty.

"Good. Now then, our holy Sabbath Day begins to-mar-row. This Sabbath Day will be like no other we have ever had in our lifetime."

He paused and watched the Levites and city elders as they looked at each other, looked at the captains who had fetched them, and looked back at the high priest.

The high priest took a deep breath and shouted it out. "Our rightful king lives!"

His voice echoed from wall to wall.

"Huh?"

"We have been hiding him in our house for 6 years," the high priest bellowed. "He is now 7. Things are so bad with the evil queen right now, we must make him our king and do it now."

The Levites and city elders stared at the high priest.

"He's alive?"

"We have a king?"

"Wait here until I return," the high priest shouted. "Do not move."

Everyone stood still and waited, straining their necks to see what the high priest was going to bring them.

Book 4: King Joash

A little while later, the high priest returned. He was holding one of little Joash's hands and Princess Jeho-sheba was holding the boy's other hand.

"Who are all the people?" Joash whis-pered.

"Shhhh. Be quiet and let them honor you," the high priest whis-pered to the boy.

"That's him?" someone in the crowd of leaders asked?

"He is still alive?" someone else whis-pered to whoever was next to him.

"We have a king after all."

One by one the city elders and Levites bowed with their heads to the floor to honor the little boy, their king.

Then the high priest and princess took Joash back to his 3rd floor.

"Wow," Joash said when he got back to his 3rd floor. "They all bowed to me."

"That is because you are their new king."

"This is what it feels like to be a king?"

The rest of the evening was spent with just the three of them—Joash and

Book 4: King Joash

his aunt and uncle in the boy's bedroom. They re-mem-bered old times of the past. Funny things, sad things. Exciting times, dull times. Then it was bed time.

"To-mar-row is going to be the biggest and most exciting day of your life," Princess Jeho-sheba said. "1,000s of people are going to come and make you their king. You need your rest so you will be ready for to-mar-row."

The future king knelt beside his bed and prayed. "Bless Uncle and Aunt. Bless my nurse. Bless my mommy and daddy in heaven. And God, bless my kingdom."

THINK & DO

1. Did you ever want something for a very long time and finally gave up ever having it? Perhaps it was a bicycle, a skate board, a pair of shoes, a book, a vaca-tion.

Then, did you get it after you gave up on it? How did you feel?

Book 4: King Joash

10 ~ Long Live the King

Once the boy was asleep, the high priest returned to the temple area where the city elders, Levites, and 500 guards with their captains were still assembled. He took the 5 captains into the meeting room. This time he did not lock the door.

"Here are your instructions….

"I want 100 men to guard the Sur Gate into and out of the temple area."

"Yes, sir."

"I want 100 men to guard the palace."

"Yes, sir."

"I want 100 men to guard the gate between the temple and the palace."

"Yes, sir."

"There are 2 other units of 100 men each that are not supposed to work to-mar-row. You will bring them here, and they will guard the king himself."

"Yes, sir."

Book 4: King Joash

"It is nearly midnight. You will have your soldiers back here before daylight. When the gates to the temple area are opened to the public worshippers to-mar-row morning, all 500 guards will be in place."

The high priest did not sleep that night. Neither did his wife, Princess Jeho-sheba. They sat in little Joash's room and thought back all they had gone through to keep the little king alive for 6 years until now.

2 hours before daylight, the high priest said he had to leave.

"I will wake him up at dawn," his wife said. "He will be ready as soon as you send for him." She smiled. "Purple robe and all," she added.

The high priest hurried down to the temple area. He walked around. The 5 captains saw him. "All the guards are in place."

"Good. And King David's silver shields and spears have been shined and passed out to all of them?"

"Yes."

A trumpet blast. The sun was up. The temple gates squeaked open. Worshippers began coming in. The high priest greeted them as they entered.

"What's going on? We heard soldiers marching all night."

They looked around. "They're here. The soldiers came here. What's going on?"

"Come," the high priest said, "come worship and praise the Lord."

After an hour, the high priest motioned to the captains of the guards. They saluted him and closed all the gates into and out of the temple area.

The high priest disappeared into his house and moments later the trumpets blasted again. And again. And again.

The worshippers came as close to the holy temple as they were allowed to.

"What's going on?"

"What are the trumpet blasts for?"

Moments later, the high priest entered the holy area where the altar to the Lord was. He had with him a child who stepped up onto a little stage."

"Who is that?" people asked each other?

The high priest motioned for silence. Then he called out in a loud voice, "Behold! Your king! He lives!"

Gasping.

Book 4: King Joash

Staring.

Tears.

Gawking.

Laughter.

The high priest moved around so he was behind the boy. He held the golden crown high above his head, then slowly lowered it onto the head of 7-year-old Joash.

"The king lives!" people shouted.

"Long live the king!"

A grand chorus of Levite men began singing.

The people cheered.

The people clapped.

"Long live the king!"

Everyone was so excited.

"Long live the king!"

Everyone was so happy.

"Long live King Joash!"

Book 4: King Joash

THINK & DO

1. Think of the most exciting day of your life. Tell about it.

2. Someday our King who will never die—Jesus—will take us to heaven where we will live with him forever. What do you think it will be like?

Thank You

Thanks for reading my book! I'm so honored that you chose to spend your precious time with my characters and entrusted me to your child. You are appreciated.

I'm an independent author who relies on my readers to help spread the word about stories you enjoy. Would you take a few minutes to let your friends know on Facebook, Pinterest... wherever you hang out online?

Also, each honest review at online retailers means a lot to me and helps other readers know if this is a book they might enjoy.

I welcome contact from readers. At my website (below), you can do so. You can also sign up for my monthly newsletter (below) to be notified of new releases, half-price print books, and 99¢ ebooks.

Book 4: King Joash

Buy Your Next Child's Book Now

Check out what they are about and get an international buy link.

A CHILD'S LIFE OF CHRIST Series of 8 books
http://bit.ly/ChildsLifeOfChristSet

A CHILD'S BIBLE HEROES Series of 10 books
http://bit.ly/ChildBibleHeroes

A CHILD'S BIBLE KIDS Series of 8 books
http://bit.ly/bible-kids

A CHILD'S BIBLE LADIES series of 10 books
http://bit.ly/2qmtwaA

OLD OLD STORY SET TO OLD OLD TUNES
http://bit.ly/BibleSongBook

FUN WITH BIBLE NUMBERS: 525 Problems
http://bit.ly/FunBibleNumbers

BIBLE PUZZLES FOR YOUNG & OLD
http://bit.ly/BiblePuzzlesYoungOld

A Child's Bible Kids

About the Author

When the author was 17 some 60 years ago, she began writing her series of eight books called They Met Jesus. When she was 60, she completed it. It is now in child's form as A CHILD'S LIFE OF CHRIST.

Her four different series of children's books are most popular among grandparents and homeschoolers. But they are popular with children around the world. Her many novels and information books are popular with grownups.

Katheryn Maddox Haddad grew up in the north and now lives in Arizona where she doesn't have to shovel sunshine. She basks in 100-degree weather with palm trees, cacti, and a computer with most of the letters worn off.

Her newspaper column appeared for several years in newspapers in Texas and North Carolina – "Little Known Facts about the Bible."

She spends half her day writing, and the other half teaching English over the internet worldwide using the Bible as textbook. Students she has converted to Christianity are hiding all over the Middle East. "They are my heroes," she declares.

Each morning she sends out an inspirational scripture thought to over 30,000 people worldwide.

She is a member of Christian Writers of the West, American Christian Fiction Writers, Historical Novel Society, and the Phoenix Screen Writers Association.

Book 4: King Joash

Connect with the Author

Website: https://inspirationsbykatheryn.com

Facebook: https://bit.ly/FacebooksKatherynMaddoxHaddad

Linkedin: http://bit.ly/KatherynLinkedin

Twitter: https://twitter.com/KatherynHaddad

Pinterest: https://www.pinterest.com/haddad1940/

Goodreads: https://www.goodreads.com/katherynmaddoxhaddad

Get a Free Book

Sign up for Katheryn's monthly newsletter with half-price books for the whole family and insider tips on what's coming next.   http://bit.ly/katheryn

Join My Dream Team

Members get the first peek at my newest book and have fun offering me advice sometimes. I have a point system of rewards for helping me get the word out. Check it out here:
http://bit.ly/KatherynsDreamTeam

www.ingramcontent.com/pod-product-compliance
Lightning Source LLC
Chambersburg PA
CBHW071537080526
44588CB00011B/1699